D0111261

It's all about…

FANTASTIC
FLIERS

KINGFISHER
NEW YORK

KINGFISHER
LONDON & NEW YORK

Copyright © Macmillan Publishers International Ltd 2016
Published in the United States by Kingfisher,
175 Fifth Ave., New York, NY 10010
Kingfisher is an imprint of Macmillan Children's Books, London
All rights reserved.

Distributed in the U.S. and Canada by Macmillan,
175 Fifth Ave., New York, NY 10010

Library of Congress Cataloging-in-Publication data
has been applied for.

Series editor: Sarah Snashall
Series design: Anthony Hannant (LittleRedAnt)
Adapted from an original text by Chris Oxlade

ISBN 978-0-7534-7286-6

Kingfisher books are available for special promotions
and premiums. For details contact: Special Markets
Department, Macmillan, 175 Fifth Ave.,
New York, NY 10010.

For more information, please visit
www.kingfisherbooks.com

Printed in China

9 8 7 6 5 4 3 2 1

1TR/0516/WKT/UG/128MA

Picture credits
The Publisher would like to thank the following for permission to reproduce their material.
Top = t; Bottom = b; Center = c; Left = l; Right = r
Cover, p1 Shutterstock/speedimaging; Back cover Shutterstock/IM_Photo; Pages 2–3, 30–31
Shutterstock/ID1974; 4 Shutterstock/Targn Pleiades; 5t Shutterstock/Mircea Bexergheanu;
5b Shutterstock/Jaggat Rishidi; 6–7 Alamy/Everett Historical; 8–9 Shutterstock/WojciechBeczynski;
9 Shutterstock/Nadezda Murmakova; 10 Alamy/Paul John Fearn; 11t Shutterstock/Zzvet;
11b Shutterstock/Tupungato; 12 Shutterstock/Carlos E Santa Maria; 13t Shutterstock/Oleg Yarko;
13b Alamy/Erik Tham; 14 Shutterstock/verzellenberg; 15 Alamy/Stocktrek Images; 16–17, 20
Shutterstock/Everett Historical; 17t Shutterstock/IanC66; 17b, 32 Shutterstock/Mauvries; 18 Alamy/
Graham Morley Historical; 19t Shutterstock/Carlos Wunderlein; 19b Shutterstock/Keith Tarrier;
21t Shutterstock/Ventura; 22–23 Shutterstock/Stefano Carnevall; 23t Shutterstock/Lukasz Janyst;
23b Shutterstock/Alexandra Lande; 24 Alamy/Ladi Kirn; 25t Shutterstock/betto rodriguez;
25b Shutterstock/David Brimm; 26 Shutterstock/Paul Drabot; 27 Alamy/AfriPics.com;
27c Shutterstock/gil80; 28 NASA; 29 Getty/Bloomberg; 29t Shutterstock/Eugene Berman.
Cards: Front tl NASA; tr Getty/Underwood Archives; bl Shutterstock/MediaVault; br Alamy/Stocktrek
Images; Back tl Shutterstock/IanC66; tr NASA; bl Alamy/Graham Morley Historic Photos;
br Shutterstock/Eugene Berman.

Front cover: The British Red Arrows aerobatic display team in action.

CONTENTS

Higher and faster

Since the beginning of time, people have looked at birds and wanted to fly. For hundreds of years, inventors tried to fly with wings or flapping machines with little success.

Birds have hollow bones, strong muscles, and air-catching feathers.

Today, modern airplanes fly higher, faster, and more safely than the early inventors could ever have dreamed.

Kites are very simple flying machines.

A modern airliner takes off with more than 300 passengers on board.

The first flight

In 1903, Orville Wright made the first-ever flight in a plane with an engine in North Carolina. The plane was called *Flyer*, and it looked more like a kite than a plane.

Flyer's first flight lasted only a few seconds but it worked!

The *Spirit of St Louis*, flown by Charles Lindbergh, was the first plane to fly from New York to Paris.

FACT...

In 1909, Louis Blériot became the first person to fly across the English Channel.

the Wright brothers' *Flyer*

SPOTLIGHT: Flyer

Famous for: first flight with an engine
Built by: Orville and Wilbur Wright
First flight: December 14, 1903
Top speed: 30 mph (48km/h)

drag

lift

How a plane flies

There are four forces (pushes and pulls)
on a plane when it is flying. When a
plane is moving at a constant speed in a
straight line, the forces are balanced. As
the speed changes, the forces also change.

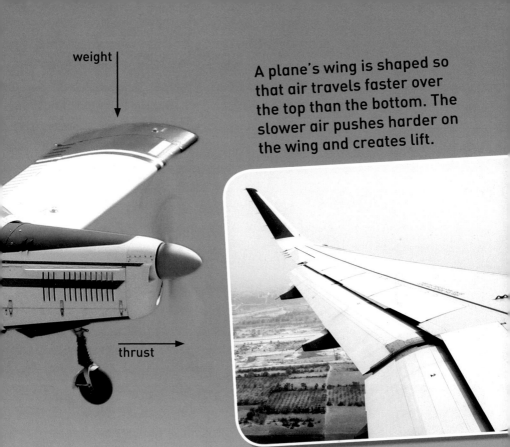

weight

A plane's wing is shaped so that air travels faster over the top than the bottom. The slower air pushes harder on the wing and creates lift.

thrust

Lift: At speed, the air under the wing pushes the plane upward.

Thrust: The engine pushes the plane forward.

Weight: This force pulls the plane downward.

Drag: The air around the plane pulls it backward.

Propeller or jet?

All planes, except gliders, have an engine. Small planes have propeller engines. These engines make a propeller spin very fast, like a giant fan.

The propeller pushes on the air, which moves the plane along.

FACT ...

The biggest jet engine ever made is the General Electric GE90. Its fan measures nearly 11 feet (3.25 meters) across.

Exhaust gases stream out of the jet engines of these fighter planes.

Most large or fast planes have jet engines. Instead of having propellers, these engines make a stream of gas.

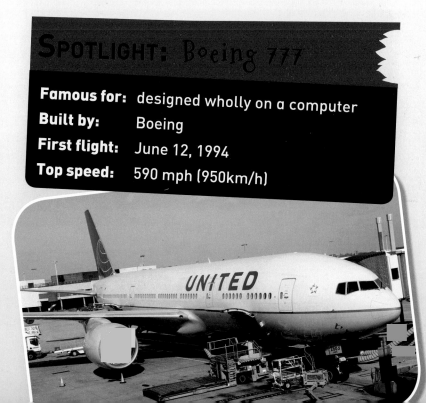

SPOTLIGHT: Boeing 777

Famous for:	designed wholly on a computer
Built by:	Boeing
First flight:	June 12, 1994
Top speed:	590 mph (950km/h)

11

Inside the cockpit

The cockpit of a plane is full of handles, pedals, switches, and dials. The pilot steers with a stick called the control column and two pedals. These make the plane climb upward, descend, turn, or bank. A handle called the throttle makes the engines go faster or slower.

FACT ...

Some military spy planes are flown by remote control. The pilot controls the plane from the ground.

The safe movement of planes across the skies is organized by the local air traffic control.

Takeoff and landing

To take off, a plane travels faster and faster down the runway until it lifts into the air.

When the plane is ready to land, the pilot slows it down and lowers the landing gear. As the wheels touch the runway, the engines go into reverse to stop the plane.

Planes must be moving very fast to take off.

Famous for:	vertical takeoff
Built by:	various manufacturers
First flight:	December 28, 1967
Top speed:	660 mph (1065km/h)

FACT ...

Some planes, such as the Harrier Jump Jet, can take off vertically. They are used on huge ships called aircraft carriers.

15

Planes at war

Many of the world's fastest and most modern planes are built by the military (armies, navies, and air forces). These planes are built to fly very quickly, to take off in difficult situations, and sometimes to be "invisible."

FACT . . .

Stealth planes, such as this *B-2 Spirit*, are designed to be almost invisible to radar.

The *Spitfire* was used by the British Royal Air Force during World War II.

SPOTLIGHT: Supermarine Spitfire

Famous for:	much-used World War II plane
Built by:	Supermarine
First flight:	March 5, 1936
Top speed:	360 mph (584km/h)

These fighter training planes can fly in formation at speeds of up to 560 miles (900 kilometers) per hour.

17

Faster than sound

The fastest planes are supersonic planes: they can fly faster than the speed of sound. Most supersonic aircraft are fighter planes, but there were two supersonic airliners: *Concorde* and *Tupolev*. *Concorde* flew higher and faster than any other airliner.

FACT ...

When a plane breaks the sound barrier, a sonic boom or bang is heard on the ground.

A cloud forms around a plane at the moment that it breaks the sound barrier.

SPOTLIGHT: SR-71 "Blackbird"

Famous for:	fastest piloted jet
Built by:	Lockheed
First flight:	December 22, 1964
Top speed:	2193 mph (3529km/h)

The *SR-71 "Blackbird"* could travel three times faster than the speed of sound.

Famous planes

History is filled with some amazing planes—and their daring pilots! These include planes that were the first to do something and planes that do something incredible.

Amelia Earhart disappeared in 1937 while flying around the world.

The Red Arrows is a British Royal Air Force display team that performs amazing aerobatic displays.

Air Force One flies the President of the United States around the world.

Gliders

A glider is a plane without an engine. A plane with an engine tows the glider into the air on a long rope. When the glider is high up, the tow plane releases the glider, which flies gently back to the ground.

Gliders have long, thin wings to help them stay in the air for as long as possible.

FACT ...

Skilled glider pilots can use the weather to glide for up to 620 miles (1000 kilometers).

Some skydivers glide in a wingsuit before opening their parachute.

A hang-glider runs along a platform to launch. This type of glider has one fixed wing.

23

Helicopters

Helicopters are not fast and cannot travel very far, but they can take off and land without a runway, such as from the top of a building or a mountain. Helicopters are used as air ambulances, as rescue vehicles, to take workers to rigs out in the ocean, and by armies across the world.

A man is rescued from the ocean by helicopter.

SPOTLIGHT: Sikorsky Black Hawk

Famous for:	favorite U.S. Army helicopter
Built by:	Sikorsky Aircraft
First flight:	October 17, 1974
Top speed:	183 mph (294km/h)

rotor blade

rotor

tail rotor

engine

fuselage

Which job?

Most of the planes we see in the sky carry passengers but planes do many other jobs. There are planes that carry cargo, planes that fight forest fires, planes that carry fuel for other aircraft, and planes used by farmers to spray their crops.

FACT ...

The biggest airliner in the world is the *Airbus A380*. It can carry 853 passengers.

Stuntman Gene Soucy performs amazing stunts on top of his plane.

A firefighting
helicopter drops
its load of water
onto the forest
fire below.

A fighter refuels from
a tanker plane.

Into space

When a space rocket launches, rocket boosters and engines burn huge amounts of fuel to launch the rocket into space. The rocket needs to travel 32 times faster than the speed of sound to break free from the pull of Earth's gravity.

Famous for:	first reusable spacecraft
Built by:	NASA
First flight:	April 12, 1981
Top speed:	17,320 mph (27,870km/h)

FACT ...

SpaceShipTwo will carry tourists into space. It will be launched by a jet plane.

WhiteKnightTwo – jet plane

SpaceShipTwo – spacecraft

GLOSSARY

air traffic control The people who organize and guide all the planes flying in the air.

airliner A large plane that carries passengers.

bank To tilt a plane to change its direction.

cockpit The space in a plane where the pilot sits and controls the plane.

descend To fly downward.

drag A push from the air that slows down a plane.

engine A machine that pushes a plane along.

exhaust The gases that come out of an engine.

fuselage The body of a plane, shaped like a tube.

glider A plane with no engine.

gliding Flying without moving its wings (bird) or without using an engine (plane).

landing gear Aircraft wheels used for landing, takeoff, and moving on the ground.

lift An upward push made by the air under a plane's wing.

propeller An object like a fan that is turned by a plane's engine. It pushes a plane along.

radar A way of finding out the location and speed of planes and ships by sending out radio signals. The signals bounce back to give information.

remote control A way to make a machine work from a distance.

rotor Part of a machine that spins round very fast.

runway A long, wide area where planes take off and land.

skydiver A person who jumps from a plane and lands using a parachute.

spy plane A plane that flies high in the sky and photographs the ground below.

thrust The push made by a plane's engines.

INDEX